iOS 17 Essentials: Everything You Need to Know

Copyright (c) 2024 by Nicholas Crow

All rights reserved. No part of this book may be reproduced in any form or by any electronic or mechanical means, including information storage and retrieval systems, without permission in writing from the publisher, except by a reviewer who may quote brief passages in a review.

Introduction

Welcome to "iOS 17 Essentials," your comprehensive guide to mastering the latest iteration of Apple's mobile operating system. Whether you're a seasoned iPhone or iPad user or just getting started with Apple devices, this book is designed to provide you with all the essential knowledge and skills you need to navigate iOS 17 with confidence. From basic setup and navigation to advanced features and troubleshooting tips, this guide covers it all, ensuring that you get the most out of your iOS 17 experience. Get ready to unlock the full potential of your iPhone or iPad with "iOS 17 Essentials" as your go-to resource.

Chapter 1

Getting Started with iOS 17

Welcome to Chapter 1 of "iOS 17 Essentials," where we embark on a journey to unlock the full potential of your iPhone or iPad. In this chapter, we'll lay the foundation for your iOS 17 experience by guiding you through the essential steps of setting up and navigating your device.

Introduction to iOS 17:

iOS 17 represents the latest evolution of Apple's renowned mobile operating system, designed to deliver an intuitive and seamless user experience. With a focus on performance enhancements, new features, and refined aesthetics, iOS 17 empowers users to do more with their devices than ever before.

Setting up your iPhone or iPad:

We'll start by walking you through the initial setup process of your iPhone or iPad, ensuring that you're equipped with the knowledge to configure your device to suit your preferences. From choosing your language and region to connecting to Wi-Fi and signing in with your Apple ID, each step is carefully explained to streamline the setup process.

Setting up your iPhone or iPad with iOS 17 is a straightforward process that ensures your device is personalized to your preferences and ready for use. Follow these step-by-step instructions to set up your device with iOS 17:

1. Turn on your Device:

   - Press and hold the Power button until the Apple logo appears on the screen. Your device will boot up, and you'll be greeted with the "Hello" screen.

2. Choose your Language and Region:

   - Slide or tap on the screen to select your preferred language, then tap "Next."

   - Select your region or country from the list provided, then tap "Next."

3. Connect to Wi-Fi or Cellular Network:

   - If you're setting up your device at home or in an area with Wi-Fi, select your Wi-Fi network from the list and enter the password if required.

   - Alternatively, you can choose to set up your device using a cellular connection by tapping "Use Cellular Connection."

4. Set up Touch ID or Face ID (if applicable):

   - If your device supports Touch ID (fingerprint recognition) or Face ID (facial recognition), you'll be prompted to set it up for added security and convenience. Follow the on-screen instructions to register your fingerprint or face.

5. Create or Sign in with your Apple ID:

   - If you have an Apple ID, tap "Sign in with your Apple ID" and enter your credentials (Apple ID and password).

   - If you don't have an Apple ID, tap "Don't have an Apple ID or forgot it?" to create a new one.

6. Set up Siri:

   - Decide whether you want to enable Siri, Apple's virtual assistant. You can choose to set it up later if you prefer.

7. Choose your Display Settings:

   - Select your preferred Display Zoom setting (Standard or Zoomed) based on your visual preference.

   - Decide whether you want to enable True Tone display, which adjusts the color temperature of your screen based on ambient light conditions.

8. Enable or Disable Location Services:

   - Choose whether to enable Location Services, which allows apps and services to use your device's location for various purposes.

9. Set up Screen Time (optional):

    - If you want to monitor and manage your device usage, you can set up Screen Time to track your screen time, app usage, and set app limits.

10. Customize your Data & Privacy Settings:

    - Review and customize your data and privacy settings according to your preferences. You can adjust settings related to analytics, advertising, app permissions, and more.

11. Choose a Theme:

    - Select your preferred appearance theme (Light or Dark Mode) to customize the look and feel of your device's interface.

12. Complete the Setup:

    - Once you've completed the setup process and customized your preferences, tap "Get Started" to access the Home Screen and start using your device with iOS 17.

Congratulations! You've successfully set up your iPhone or iPad with iOS 17, and your device is now ready for you to explore its features and capabilities. Enjoy your iOS 17 experience!

Navigating the Home Screen and Control Center:

Navigating the iOS 17 Home Screen and Control Center on your iPhone or iPad is essential for accessing apps, settings, and functions quickly and efficiently. Here's a guide on how to navigate both:

Navigating the iOS 17 Home Screen:

1. Accessing the Home Screen:

   - Press the Home button (for iPhones with Touch ID) or swipe up from the bottom of the screen (for iPhones without a Home button) to return to the Home Screen from any app or screen.

2. App Icons:

   - App icons are displayed on the Home Screen. Tap on an app icon to launch the corresponding app.

3. App Folders:

   - Organize your apps into folders by dragging one app icon onto another. This helps keep your Home Screen organized and clutter-free.

4. App Library:

   - Swipe left on the Home Screen to access the App Library, where all your installed apps are automatically organized into categories. Tap on an app to open it or use the search bar at the top to find specific apps.

5. Widgets:

   - Widgets provide at-a-glance information and quick actions right from the Home Screen. To add a widget, long-press on an empty area of the Home Screen, tap the "+" icon in the top-left corner, select a widget, then tap "Add Widget" to add it to your Home Screen.

Navigating the iOS 17 Control Center:

1. Accessing the Control Center:

   - Swipe down from the top-right corner of the screen (iPhone with Face ID) or swipe up from the bottom of the screen (iPhone with Touch ID) to access the Control Center from any screen, including the Home Screen and within apps.

2. Control Center Modules:

   - The Control Center consists of various modules that provide quick access to commonly used settings and functions.

      - Top Row: Includes modules such as Wi-Fi, Bluetooth, Cellular Data, Airplane Mode, and Screen Mirroring.

      - Middle Row: Contains modules for controlling brightness, volume, and media playback.

      - Bottom Row: Houses additional modules like Do Not

Disturb, Screen Recording, and more.

3. Customizing the Control Center:

   - You can customize the Control Center by adding, removing, or rearranging modules to suit your preferences. Go to Settings > Control Center > Customize Controls to make changes.

4. Quick Actions and Shortcuts:

   - Many Control Center modules offer quick actions and shortcuts. For example, long-pressing on the Wi-Fi module allows you to access available Wi-Fi networks, while long-pressing on the Music module provides playback controls.

5. Dismissal:

   - To dismiss the Control Center, swipe it up or tap on an empty area of the screen.

Mastering the navigation of the iOS 17 Home Screen and Control Center allows you to navigate your iPhone or iPad with ease and efficiency, maximizing your productivity and enjoyment of your device.

Chapter 2

Mastering Basic Functions

Welcome to Chapter 2 of "iOS 17 Essentials," where we delve into mastering the basic functions of your iPhone or iPad. In this chapter, we will guide you through essential tasks such as making and receiving calls, sending text messages and iMessages, and managing your contacts and favorites.

Making and Receiving Calls:

Making and receiving calls on iOS 17 is a fundamental feature of the iPhone, providing users with a seamless and intuitive experience for staying connected with friends, family, and colleagues. Here's a detailed explanation of how to make and receive calls on iOS 17:

Making Calls:

1. Using the Phone App:

- Open the Phone app from the Home Screen.

- Tap the "Keypad" tab at the bottom of the screen to enter a phone number manually.

- Alternatively, tap the "Contacts" tab to select a contact from your address book.

- Once you've entered the number or selected a contact, tap the green call button to initiate the call.

2. Using Siri:

- Activate Siri by holding down the side button or saying "Hey Siri."

- Issue a command such as "Call [contact's name]" or "Call [phone number]."

- Siri will confirm the contact or number and initiate the call.

3. Using Favorites or Recents:

- Access your Favorites or Recents by tapping the corresponding tab in the Phone app.

- Tap on a favorite or recent contact to initiate a call directly.

4. Using FaceTime:

   - Initiate a FaceTime audio call by opening the FaceTime app or tapping the FaceTime icon in a contact's information.

   - Select the contact you want to call and tap the phone icon next to their name to start the call.

Receiving Calls:

1. Incoming Call Notifications:

   - When you receive an incoming call, your iPhone will display a notification on the Lock Screen with options to accept or decline the call.

   - You'll also see the caller's name or number displayed on the screen.

2. Answering Calls:

- To answer an incoming call, tap the green "Accept" button on the Lock Screen, or swipe right on the notification.

- If your device is unlocked when a call comes in, you'll see the notification at the top of the screen. Tap "Accept" to answer the call.

3. Declining Calls:

- To decline an incoming call, tap the red "Decline" button on the Lock Screen, or swipe left on the notification.

- You can also decline a call by pressing the side button or volume button.

4. Managing Calls:

- During a call, you can adjust the call volume using the volume buttons on the side of your device.

- To end a call, tap the red "End Call" button on the screen or press the side button.

5. Using Call Waiting:

- If you receive a second call while on a call, you'll see the option to "Hold & Accept" or "Decline" the incoming call. Tap the appropriate option to manage the calls.

Sending Text Messages and iMessages:

Sending text messages and iMessages on iOS 17 is a convenient way to communicate with friends, family, and colleagues. Here's a detailed explanation of how to send text messages and iMessages:

Sending Text Messages:

1. Using the Messages App:

   - Open the Messages app from the Home Screen.

   - Tap the compose button (usually a pencil icon) in the top-right corner to start a new message.

2. Selecting Recipients:

- Enter the recipient's phone number or select them from your contacts by typing their name in the "To:" field.

- You can also add multiple recipients to a group message by entering multiple phone numbers or selecting multiple contacts.

3. Composing the Message:

- Tap the text field at the bottom of the screen to start typing your message.

- You can also add emojis, photos, videos, and other attachments by tapping the corresponding icons next to the text field.

4. Sending the Message:

- Once you've composed your message, tap the send button (usually a blue arrow) to send it to the recipient(s).

Sending iMessages:

1. Difference Between iMessages and Text Messages:

   - iMessages are a type of message sent between Apple devices using an internet connection, such as Wi-Fi or cellular data.

   - iMessages are distinguished by their blue color in the Messages app, while regular text messages are green.

2. Ensuring iMessage is Enabled:

   - To send iMessages, ensure that iMessage is enabled on your device. Go to Settings > Messages and toggle the iMessage switch to the ON position.

3. Sending iMessages:

   - Follow the same steps as sending a text message, but ensure that the recipient's contact details are associated with an Apple ID or iCloud account.

   - If the recipient is using an Apple device with iMessage enabled, your message will be sent as an iMessage and will appear in blue.

4. iMessage Features:

   - iMessages offer additional features beyond traditional text messages, including:

      - Read receipts: See when your message has been delivered and read by the recipient.

      - Typing indicators: Know when the recipient is typing a response.

      - Tapbacks: React to messages with a thumbs up, thumbs down, heart, laugh, or question mark.

      - Digital touch: Send sketches, heartbeats, and other interactive messages.

Managing Contacts and Favorites:

Managing contacts and favorites on iOS 17 is essential for

keeping your address book organized and easily accessible. Here's a detailed explanation of how to manage contacts and favorites on your iPhone or iPad:

Managing Contacts:

1. Using the Contacts App:

    - Open the Contacts app from the Home Screen.

    - Here, you'll find your list of contacts organized alphabetically by name.

2. Adding a New Contact:

    - To add a new contact, tap the "+" icon in the top-right corner.

    - Enter the contact's name, phone number, email address, and any additional information you want to include, such as their address or birthday.

    - Tap "Done" to save the contact.

3. Editing Contacts:

   - To edit an existing contact, tap on the contact's name to open their details.

   - Tap "Edit" in the top-right corner to make changes to their information.

   - After making your edits, tap "Done" to save the changes.

4. Deleting Contacts:

   - To delete a contact, open the contact's details and scroll to the bottom.

   - Tap "Edit" and then scroll down again to find the "Delete Contact" option.

   - Confirm the deletion by tapping "Delete Contact."

5. Organizing Contacts into Groups:

   - You can organize your contacts into groups for easier management.

- Tap "Groups" at the top-left corner of the Contacts app to view your contact groups.

- To create a new group, tap "Create New" and enter a name for the group.

- To add contacts to a group, tap "Edit" while viewing the contact's details, then select the group under "Add to Existing Groups."

Managing Favorites:

1. Adding Favorites:

- Favorites are a convenient way to quickly access your most frequently contacted individuals.

- To add a contact to your Favorites, open their contact details and tap "Add to Favorites."

- Alternatively, you can swipe right on a contact in the Contacts app or Phone app and tap the star icon to add them to your Favorites.

2. Accessing Favorites:

   - To access your Favorites, open the Phone app and select the "Favorites" tab at the bottom.

   - Here, you'll find a list of your favorite contacts, making it easy to call or message them with just a tap.

3. Removing Favorites:

   - To remove a contact from your Favorites, open their contact details and tap "Remove from Favorites."

   - Alternatively, swipe right on the contact in the Favorites list and tap the star icon again to remove them.

Chapter 3

Exploring iOS 17 Features

Welcome to Chapter 3 of "iOS 17 Essentials," where we embark on a journey to explore the exciting features and functionalities of iOS 17. In this chapter, we'll dive deep into the various tools and enhancements that iOS 17 offers, empowering you to make the most out of your iPhone or iPad experience.

Siri and Voice Commands:

Siri is Apple's intelligent virtual assistant, designed to help users perform tasks, access information, and control their devices using natural language voice commands. In iOS 17, Siri continues to evolve, offering new features and capabilities to enhance the user experience. Here's a detailed explanation of Siri and how to use voice commands on iOS 17:

Activating Siri:

- There are several ways to activate Siri on your iPhone or iPad:

    - Press and hold the side button (on devices with Face ID) or the Home button (on devices with Touch ID).

    - Say "Hey Siri" followed by your command, if Hey Siri is enabled in your settings.

Issuing Voice Commands:

- Once Siri is activated, you can issue voice commands to perform a wide range of tasks, including:

    - Sending messages: "Send a message to [contact] saying I'm running late."

    - Making calls: "Call [contact] on speakerphone."

    - Setting reminders and alarms: "Remind me to buy milk at 6 p.m."

    - Getting directions: "Give me directions to the nearest coffee shop."

    - Playing music: "Play my workout playlist."

    - Checking the weather: "What's the weather like today?"

- Getting answers to questions: "How many ounces are in a cup?"

Siri Shortcuts:

- Siri Shortcuts allow you to create custom voice commands for automating tasks and workflows on your device.

- You can create shortcuts for actions within apps or combine multiple actions into a single shortcut.

- For example, you could create a shortcut called "Heading Home" that sends a text to your spouse, starts navigation to your home address, and adjusts your home thermostat—all with a single voice command.

Customizing Siri:

- You can customize Siri's settings to personalize your experience and tailor Siri's responses to your preferences.

- Go to Settings > Siri & Search to adjust settings such as voice feedback, language, and Siri Suggestions.

Privacy and Security:

- Apple prioritizes user privacy and security, and Siri is designed with these principles in mind.

- Siri interactions are processed on-device whenever possible, meaning that your voice commands are not sent to Apple's servers unless necessary for processing.

- You can review and manage your Siri and dictation history in Settings > Siri & Search > Siri & Dictation History.

Spotlight Search:

Spotlight Search is a powerful feature on iOS 17 that allows users to quickly find information, apps, contacts, and more on their iPhone or iPad. It provides a convenient way to access content and perform tasks without navigating through multiple menus or opening specific apps. Here's an explanation of how Spotlight Search works and how to use it effectively:

Accessing Spotlight Search:

- Swipe down from the middle of the Home Screen to access Spotlight Search.

- Alternatively, you can swipe right on the Home Screen to access the Today View, then swipe down to reveal the search bar at the top.

Search Suggestions:

- As you start typing in the search bar, Spotlight Search provides search suggestions based on your query.

- These suggestions may include apps, contacts, recent documents, websites, and more, making it easier to find what you're looking for.

Refining Search Results:

- You can refine your search results by using keywords, filters, and modifiers.

- For example, typing "weather" will display the current weather forecast for your location, while typing "email from [contact]" will show you recent emails from that contact.

Actions and Shortcuts:

- Spotlight Search also provides quick actions and shortcuts for common tasks.

- For example, you can use Spotlight Search to:

    - Call or message a contact by typing their name.

    - Open apps by typing their name or initials.

    - Perform calculations by typing mathematical expressions.

    - Find nearby locations by typing "restaurants near me" or "gas stations nearby."

Searching Within Apps:

- Spotlight Search can also search within apps to help you find specific content.

- For example, you can search for emails, messages, notes, files, and more directly from Spotlight Search.

Customization:

- You can customize Spotlight Search settings to control which types of content are included in search results.

- Go to Settings > Siri & Search to manage search suggestions, app suggestions, and more.

Privacy and Security:

- Apple prioritizes user privacy and security, and Spotlight Search is designed to respect user privacy.

- Your search queries are processed locally on your device, meaning that your personal information is not shared with Apple or third parties.

Notifications and Do Not Disturb:

Notifications and Do Not Disturb are two features on iOS 17 designed to manage incoming notifications and help users stay focused and undisturbed when needed. Here's an explanation of how these features work and how to use them effectively:

Notifications:

1. Types of Notifications:

   - Notifications on iOS 17 can come from various sources, including apps, messages, emails, calendar events, and more.

   - They can appear as banners, alerts, or badges on the Lock Screen, Home Screen, or within apps.

2. Managing Notifications:

   - You can customize notification settings for each app to control how and when you receive notifications.

   - Go to Settings > Notifications to manage notification preferences for individual apps.

   - Here, you can enable or disable notifications, choose the notification style (banners, alerts, or none), and adjust notification sounds and badges.

3. Notification Center:

- Swipe down from the top of the screen to access the Notification Center, where you can view and interact with your notifications.

- Notifications are grouped by app and can be cleared individually or all at once.

4. Notification Actions:

- Some notifications include actions that allow you to interact with them directly, such as replying to a message or snoozing a reminder.

Do Not Disturb:

1. Enabling Do Not Disturb:

- Do Not Disturb is a feature that silences incoming calls, messages, and notifications to minimize interruptions.

- You can enable Do Not Disturb manually or schedule it to activate automatically during specific times.

- Swipe down from the top of the screen to access Control

Center, then tap the crescent moon icon to enable Do Not Disturb.

- To schedule Do Not Disturb, go to Settings > Do Not Disturb and set the desired schedule.

2. Customizing Do Not Disturb:

- You can customize Do Not Disturb settings to allow certain notifications to come through while in Do Not Disturb mode.

- Go to Settings > Do Not Disturb to adjust settings such as allowing calls from specific contacts, allowing repeated calls to ring through, and enabling Bedtime Mode.

3. Do Not Disturb While Driving:

- iOS 17 includes a feature called "Do Not Disturb While Driving," which automatically detects when you're driving and silences notifications to help minimize distractions.

- You can enable this feature manually or have it activate automatically when your iPhone detects that you're driving.

Chapter 4

Using Built-in Apps

Welcome to Chapter 4 of "iOS 17 Essentials," where we explore the built-in apps that come pre-installed on your iPhone or iPad. In this chapter, we'll delve into the functionalities of essential apps like Safari, Mail, and Maps, empowering you to browse the web, manage your email, and navigate with ease using iOS 17.

Safari: Browsing the Web

Safari is Apple's native web browser, designed to provide a fast, secure, and user-friendly browsing experience on iOS devices. Here's a detailed explanation of how to use Safari for browsing the web on iOS 17:

1. Navigation and Tabs:

- Safari allows you to navigate the web with ease using tabs.

- To open a new tab, tap the tab icon (usually a square with a number inside) in the top-right corner of the screen, then tap the "+" button.

- You can switch between tabs by tapping on them or swiping left and right across the tab bar.

2. Browsing Websites:

- Enter a website URL or search query in the address bar at the top of the screen.

- Safari will suggest search results and website URLs as you type, making it easy to find what you're looking for.

- Tap on a search result or website URL to open it in the current tab.

3. Reader View:

- Safari's Reader View removes distractions from web pages, such as ads and formatting, to provide a clean and easy-to-read view of the content.

- Tap the Reader View icon in the address bar (usually a set of lines) to activate Reader View for compatible web pages.

4. Bookmarks and History:

- Safari allows you to save your favorite websites as bookmarks for easy access.

- Tap the bookmarks icon (usually a book) in the toolbar to view your bookmarks and browsing history.

- You can add a website to your bookmarks by tapping the share icon (usually a square with an arrow pointing up) and selecting "Add Bookmark."

5. Content Blockers:

- Safari supports content blockers, which are third-party apps that can block advertisements, trackers, and other unwanted content from websites.

- You can install content blockers from the App Store and enable them in Safari settings to enhance your browsing experience.

6. Privacy and Security:

- Safari prioritizes user privacy and security, with features like Intelligent Tracking Prevention (ITP) to prevent cross-site tracking.

- Your browsing history and website data are stored locally on your device by default, but you can choose to clear this data in Safari settings for enhanced privacy.

7. Additional Features:

- Safari offers additional features such as Reader View, Reading List for saving articles to read later, and iCloud Tabs for syncing open tabs across your devices.

Mail: Managing Email Accounts

The Mail app on iOS 17 is a powerful tool for managing your email accounts, allowing you to stay connected and organized while on the go. Here's a detailed explanation of how to manage email accounts using the Mail app:

1. Setting Up Email Accounts:

- To get started, open the Mail app from your Home Screen.

- Tap "Add Account" and select your email service provider (e.g., iCloud, Google, Yahoo, Outlook).

- Follow the on-screen instructions to sign in to your email account and configure the necessary settings.

2. Composing and Sending Emails:

- To compose a new email, tap the compose button (usually a pencil icon) in the bottom-right corner of the screen.

- Enter the recipient's email address, subject, and message content.

- You can also add attachments, such as photos, videos, and documents, by tapping the paperclip icon.

3. Managing Email Folders:

- The Mail app organizes your emails into folders such as Inbox, Sent, Drafts, and Trash.

- You can create custom folders to further organize your emails by tapping "Edit" in the Mailboxes view and selecting "New Mailbox."

4. Reading and Responding to Emails:

- Tap on an email in your Inbox to read its contents.

- Swipe left on an email to reveal options such as Reply, Forward, Archive, Flag, and Delete.

- Tap "Reply" to respond to the email, "Forward" to send it to another recipient, or "Archive" to move it to the Archive folder.

5. Customizing Email Settings:

- You can customize various email settings in the Mail app to tailor it to your preferences.

- Go to Settings > Mail to adjust settings such as notification preferences, signature, swipe actions, and mail fetch frequency.

6. Managing Multiple Email Accounts:

- The Mail app allows you to manage multiple email accounts in one place.

- To switch between email accounts, tap the mailbox icon in the top-left corner of the Mail app and select the desired account.

7. Synchronization and Notifications:

- The Mail app automatically syncs your emails across all your devices connected to the same email account.

- You can enable or disable email notifications for each account in Settings > Mail > Notifications.

8. Security and Privacy:

- Apple prioritizes user security and privacy, and the Mail app is designed with these principles in mind.

- Your email data is encrypted and stored securely on your device, and Apple does not have access to the contents of your emails.

Maps: Navigation and Location Services

Maps is Apple's native mapping and navigation app, offering comprehensive location services and turn-by-turn directions to help users navigate with ease on their iPhone or iPad. Here's a detailed explanation of how to use Maps for navigation and location services on iOS 17:

1. Searching for Locations:

- Open the Maps app from your Home Screen.

- Enter the name or address of the location you want to find in the search bar at the top of the screen.

- Maps will provide search suggestions and auto-complete options as you type, making it easy to find the location you're looking for.

2. Getting Directions:

- Once you've found your desired location, tap on it to view more details.

- Tap the "Directions" button to get turn-by-turn directions to the location from your current location.

- You can choose between driving, walking, or public transit directions, depending on your mode of transportation.

3. Turn-by-Turn Navigation:

- Maps provides turn-by-turn navigation with spoken instructions to guide you to your destination.

- Follow the highlighted route on the map and listen to the voice prompts for upcoming turns and directions.

- Maps also offers real-time traffic information and alternative routes to help you avoid congestion and delays.

4. Exploring Maps Features:

- Maps offers additional features to enhance your navigation experience, such as:

    - Satellite view: View detailed satellite imagery of locations.

    - 3D Flyover: Explore select cities and landmarks in immersive 3D.

- Share ETA: Share your estimated time of arrival with friends or family members.

- Indoor Maps: Navigate indoor spaces like airports, malls, and transit stations with detailed indoor maps.

5. Location Services:

- Maps relies on location services to provide accurate navigation and directions.

- Ensure that location services are enabled for Maps by going to Settings > Privacy > Location Services and toggling the switch next to Maps.

- You can also customize location permissions for Maps, such as allowing location access only while using the app.

6. Privacy and Security:

- Apple prioritizes user privacy and security, and Maps is designed with these principles in mind.

- Your location data is anonymized and encrypted when using Maps, and Apple does not store a history of your location searches or navigation routes.

Chapter 5

Enhancing Productivity with iOS 17

Welcome to Chapter 5 of "iOS 17 Essentials," where we explore how iOS 17 empowers users to enhance their productivity and efficiency. In this chapter, we'll delve into a range of features and tools that streamline workflows, optimize organization, and boost productivity on your iPhone or iPad.

1. Reminders:

The Reminders app on iOS 17 is a powerful tool designed to help users stay organized and on top of their tasks, commitments, and to-do lists. Here's a detailed explanation of how to use Reminders effectively:

1. Creating Reminders:

- Open the Reminders app from your Home Screen.

- Tap the "+" button in the top-right corner to create a new reminder.

- Enter the title of your reminder and tap "Return" to add it to your list.

- You can also set due dates, times, and locations for your reminders to receive notifications and alerts when they're due.

2. Managing Lists:

- Reminders allows you to organize your tasks into lists for easy access and organization.

- Tap "Add List" to create a new list, and give it a name that reflects its purpose (e.g., Work, Personal, Groceries).

- You can switch between lists by tapping on them from the main Reminders screen.

3. Setting Priorities:

- You can prioritize your reminders by assigning them priority levels (High, Medium, Low) or by adding flags.

- Tap the "i" icon next to a reminder to view and edit its details, including priority, due date, and notes.

4. Smart Suggestions:

- Reminders offers smart suggestions based on context, location, and time to help you stay organized.

- For example, if you type "Call" followed by a contact's name, Reminders may suggest setting a reminder to call that person.

5. Siri Integration:

- Siri integration allows you to create and manage reminders using voice commands.

- Activate Siri by holding down the side button or saying "Hey Siri," then issue a command such as "Remind me to buy milk when I get to the grocery store."

6. Shared Lists:

- Reminders allows you to share lists with family members, friends, or colleagues for collaborative task management.

- Tap the "Add List" button, then select "Add People" to invite others to view and edit the list.

7. Notification and Alerts:

- Reminders sends notifications and alerts to remind you of upcoming tasks and deadlines.

- You can customize notification settings for each reminder, including the time and type of notification (e.g., banners, alerts, sounds).

8. Completing and Managing Reminders:

- When you've completed a task, tap the checkbox next to the reminder to mark it as complete.

- Completed reminders are moved to the bottom of the list and can be viewed in the "Completed" section.

- You can also delete or edit reminders by swiping left on them and tapping the appropriate action.

2. Notes:

The Notes app on iOS 17 is a versatile tool designed to help users capture ideas, jot down thoughts, and organize information in a convenient and intuitive manner. Here's a detailed explanation of how to use Notes effectively:

1. Creating and Formatting Notes:

- Open the Notes app from your Home Screen.

- Tap the "+" button in the bottom-right corner to create a new note.

- Enter your text, and use the formatting toolbar at the bottom of the screen to format your text, including options such as bold, italics, underline, bullet points, and numbering.

2. Adding Media and Attachments:

- Notes allows you to enrich your notes with multimedia content and attachments.

- Tap the "+" button above the keyboard to access additional options, such as adding photos, videos, sketches, scanned documents, and website links to your note.

3. Organizing Notes:

- Notes offers various organizational features to help you keep your notes organized and easily accessible.

- You can create folders to categorize your notes by topic, project, or theme.

- Swipe left on a note to reveal options for organizing, pinning, or deleting it.

4. Collaboration and Sharing:

- Notes supports collaboration, allowing you to share notes with others and work together in real-time.

- Tap the share icon at the top of a note to invite others to collaborate via iCloud sharing.

- You can grant permissions for viewing or editing, and collaborators can add comments, make edits, and contribute to the note.

5. Searching and Navigation:

- Notes offers powerful search capabilities to help you find specific notes quickly.

- Tap the search bar at the top of the Notes app and enter keywords to search for notes containing those terms.

- Notes also provides a list view and grid view for navigating your notes, making it easy to find what you're looking for.

6. Security and Privacy:

- Apple prioritizes user security and privacy, and Notes is designed with these principles in mind.

- Your notes are encrypted and stored securely on your device and in iCloud, ensuring that your personal information remains protected.

- You can enable Face ID, Touch ID, or a password to lock individual notes for an extra layer of security.

7. Integration with Other Apps:

- Notes seamlessly integrates with other apps and services on iOS, allowing you to share content between apps and access your notes from various devices.

- You can use the Share Sheet to send content from other apps directly to Notes, or use the Notes app extension to create notes from Safari, Maps, Photos, and more.

3. Calendar:

The Calendar app on iOS 17 is a powerful tool designed to help users stay organized and manage their schedules effectively. Here's a detailed explanation of how to use Calendar effectively:

1. Creating Events:

- Open the Calendar app from your Home Screen.

- Tap the "+" button in the top-right corner to create a new event.

- Enter the event details, including the title, location, date, and time.

- You can also set reminders and alerts to receive notifications before the event starts.

2. Managing Events:

- Calendar allows you to view and manage your events by day, week, month, or year.

- Tap on a date to view its events, or switch between views by tapping the corresponding tabs at the bottom of the screen.

- You can edit or delete events by tapping on them and selecting the appropriate action.

3. Adding Invitations:

- Calendar supports event invitations, allowing you to invite others to your events and track RSVPs.

- Tap the "+" button when creating a new event, then tap "Invitees" to add attendees from your contacts.

- Invited attendees will receive an invitation via email or calendar notification, and their responses will be updated in the event details.

4. Syncing with Other Calendars:

- Calendar syncs with other calendars and services, such as iCloud, Google Calendar, and Microsoft Exchange.

- You can add and manage multiple calendars within the Calendar app, allowing you to keep track of personal, work, and shared calendars in one place.

5. Natural Language Input:

- Calendar offers natural language input, allowing you to create events using plain language.

- For example, you can type "Meeting with John tomorrow at 2 PM" to create a new event for the following day at 2 PM with the title "Meeting with John."

6. iCloud Syncing:

- Calendar syncs your events and appointments across all your devices using iCloud.

- Ensure that iCloud syncing is enabled in Settings > [your name] >

iCloud > Calendar to keep your calendars up to date across your iPhone, iPad, Mac, and other iCloud-enabled devices.

7. Location-Based Suggestions:

- Calendar provides location-based suggestions when creating events, helping you quickly find and select relevant locations for your appointments.

- Tap the location field when creating a new event to view nearby places and select the desired location from the suggestions.

8. Time Zone Support:

- Calendar offers time zone support, allowing you to create events and view appointments in different time zones.

- When traveling or scheduling events across time zones, Calendar will automatically adjust event times to match your current location.

4. Files:

The Files app on iOS 17 is a comprehensive file management tool designed to help users organize, access, and manage their documents, photos, videos, and other files. Here's a detailed explanation of how to use Files effectively:

1. Browsing Files and Folders:

- Open the Files app from your Home Screen.

- Navigate through your files and folders using the sidebar on the left-hand side of the screen.

- Tap on a folder to view its contents, and tap on a file to preview it.

2. Searching for Files:

- Files offers a powerful search feature to help you find specific files quickly.

- Tap the search bar at the top of the screen and enter keywords to search for files containing those terms.

- Files also provides suggestions and filters to refine your search results.

3. Organizing Files:

- Files allows you to organize your files and folders in a variety of ways.

- You can create new folders by tapping the "+" button in the sidebar and selecting "New Folder."

- Drag and drop files and folders to rearrange them or move them to different locations within the Files app.

4. Viewing and Editing Documents:

- Files supports a wide range of file types, allowing you to view and edit documents, spreadsheets, presentations, images, videos, and more.

- Tap on a compatible file to preview it, and use the built-in document viewer to read, annotate, or edit the file.

- You can also open files in their respective apps for more advanced editing capabilities.

5. iCloud Integration:

- Files seamlessly integrates with iCloud, allowing you to access your files across all your devices.

- Your files are automatically synced to iCloud, ensuring that you have access to the latest versions of your documents and files on your iPhone, iPad, Mac, and other iCloud-enabled devices.

6. Integration with Third-Party Services:

- Files supports integration with third-party cloud storage services such as Dropbox, Google Drive, and OneDrive.

- You can add accounts from these services to Files and access your files stored in the cloud directly from the app.

7. Tagging and Favorites:

- Files allows you to tag files and folders to categorize and organize them more effectively.

- You can also mark files and folders as favorites to access them quickly from the Favorites section in the sidebar.

8. Sharing and Collaboration:

- Files supports sharing and collaboration, allowing you to share files and folders with others and work together in real-time.

- Tap the share icon next to a file or folder to share it via AirDrop, Messages, Mail, or other apps.

5. Screen Time:

Screen Time is a feature on iOS 17 designed to help users understand and manage their device usage habits, promote healthy screen time habits, and reduce distractions. Here's a detailed explanation of how to use Screen Time effectively:

1. Understanding Usage Data:

- Screen Time provides insights into how much time you spend on your iPhone or iPad and which apps you use the most.

- Open the Settings app from your Home Screen and tap "Screen Time" to view your usage data.

- You'll see a summary of your screen time, including total screen time, time spent on each app, pickups, notifications received, and more.

2. Setting App Limits:

- Screen Time allows you to set time limits for specific apps or app categories to help you manage your usage and avoid spending too much time on certain activities.

- Tap "App Limits" in the Screen Time settings to set limits for categories such as Social Networking, Games, Entertainment, and more.

- Once you reach your time limit for a particular app or category, Screen Time will notify you and restrict access to the app until the next day.

3. Downtime:

- Downtime is a feature that allows you to schedule periods of time when you want to take a break from screen time and focus on other activities.

- Tap "Downtime" in the Screen Time settings to schedule downtime for specific times of the day.

- During downtime, only apps that you've allowed in the Always Allowed list will be accessible, such as Phone, Messages, and certain educational apps.

4. App Restrictions:

- Screen Time allows you to restrict access to certain apps or features, such as in-app purchases, explicit content, and Siri.

- Tap "Content & Privacy Restrictions" in the Screen Time settings to set restrictions for specific apps, features, and content types.

- You can also set up a Screen Time passcode to prevent unauthorized changes to your Screen Time settings.

5. Communication Limits:

- Communication Limits allow you to manage who you can communicate with during certain times, such as during Downtime or Bedtime.

- Tap "Communication Limits" in the Screen Time settings to set limits for who you can communicate with via Phone, FaceTime, Messages, and iCloud Contacts.

- You can specify contacts that are always allowed, or create exceptions for specific contacts.

6. Screen Time for Family:

- Screen Time offers Family Sharing features, allowing parents to monitor and manage their children's device usage.

- Parents can view their children's Screen Time data, set app limits, schedule downtime, and manage content restrictions remotely from their own devices.

Chapter 6

Customizing Your Device

Customizing your iPhone or iPad on iOS 17 allows you to tailor your device to suit your preferences, style, and workflow. From changing wallpapers to adjusting accessibility settings, iOS 17 offers a wide range of customization options to enhance your user experience. Here's a detailed guide on how to customize your device effectively:

1. Personalizing the Home Screen:

- Start by personalizing your Home Screen with your favorite apps, widgets, and wallpapers.

- To change your wallpaper, go to Settings > Wallpaper > Choose a New Wallpaper, and select from the available options, including dynamic, still, and Live wallpapers.

- Arrange your apps and create folders to organize them based on categories or usage frequency.

2. Customizing Control Center:

- Control Center provides quick access to essential settings and features, and you can customize it to include the controls you use most frequently.

- Go to Settings > Control Center to add, remove, or rearrange controls such as Wi-Fi, Bluetooth, AirDrop, and Screen Recording.

3. Adjusting Display and Brightness Settings:

- Customize your display and brightness settings to suit your preferences and optimize battery life.

- Go to Settings > Display & Brightness to adjust settings such as brightness level, True Tone, Night Shift, and auto-lock duration.

4. Personalizing Sounds and Haptics:

- Customize your device's sounds, vibrations, and haptic feedback to reflect your personal style.

- Go to Settings > Sounds & Haptics to adjust settings such as ringtones, vibrations, and system haptics.

5. Configuring Accessibility Settings:

- iOS 17 offers a range of accessibility features to accommodate different needs and preferences.

- Go to Settings > Accessibility to customize settings such as text size, display accommodations, color filters, and assistive touch.

6. Setting up Siri and Search Preferences:

- Customize Siri and Search preferences to enhance your voice assistant experience.

- Go to Settings > Siri & Search to enable or disable Siri, customize voice feedback, and manage Siri suggestions.

7. Managing Privacy and Security Settings:

- Take control of your privacy and security settings to protect your personal information and data.

- Go to Settings > Privacy & Security to manage settings such as location services, app permissions, and advertising tracking.

8. Exploring Additional Customization Options:

- iOS 17 offers additional customization options to explore, such as app-specific settings, keyboard preferences, and Siri shortcuts.

- Dive into the settings of your favorite apps to discover additional customization options and features.

Chapter 7

Entertainment and Media: Enhancing Your Experience on iOS 17

In the digital age, iOS 17 offers a wealth of entertainment and media options to keep you entertained, informed, and inspired. From streaming your favorite movies and TV shows to discovering new music and podcasts, iOS 17 transforms your iPhone or iPad into a versatile entertainment hub. Here's a detailed guide on how to make the most of entertainment and media on iOS 17:

1. Streaming Services:

- iOS 17 provides access to a variety of streaming services, including Apple TV+, Netflix, Hulu, Disney+, Spotify, and Apple Music.

- Download the apps from the App Store and sign up for subscriptions to stream a vast library of movies, TV shows, music, and podcasts.

- Explore curated recommendations, personalized playlists, and exclusive content tailored to your preferences and interests.

2. Apple TV App:

- The Apple TV app on iOS 17 offers a seamless viewing experience, allowing you to discover, rent, purchase, and watch movies and TV shows from various sources in one place.

- Browse through a wide selection of content, including Apple Originals, blockbuster movies, and trending TV shows.

- Enjoy features such as personalized recommendations, family sharing, and offline downloads for on-the-go viewing.

3. Gaming:

- iOS 17 is home to a vibrant gaming ecosystem, with thousands of games available for download from the App Store.

- Discover a diverse range of gaming experiences, from casual puzzle games to immersive multiplayer adventures.

- Take advantage of features such as Game Center, iCloud save syncing, and controller support to enhance your gaming experience on iOS 17.

4. Reading and News:

- iOS 17 offers access to a plethora of reading and news apps, including Apple News, Kindle, Audible, and Scribd.

- Stay informed and entertained with personalized news articles, audiobooks, e-books, and digital magazines.

- Customize your reading experience with features such as font size adjustment, night mode, and bookmarking.

5. Podcasts:

- Podcasts have become increasingly popular on iOS 17, with a wide selection of shows covering diverse topics and genres.

- Explore podcasts on technology, comedy, true crime, storytelling, and more.

- Subscribe to your favorite podcasts, download episodes for offline listening, and discover new shows through recommendations and curated playlists.

6. Social Media and Sharing:

- Stay connected with friends and family and share your favorite moments using social media apps such as Instagram, Snapchat, Facebook, and Twitter.

- Create and share photos, videos, stories, and live broadcasts to engage with your audience and express yourself creatively.

- Discover trending topics, join communities, and connect with like-minded individuals from around the world.

7. Creative Tools:

- iOS 17 offers a variety of creative tools and apps to unleash your artistic talents and express your creativity.

- Explore apps such as Procreate, Adobe Creative Cloud, and GarageBand to create digital art, edit photos and videos, compose music, and more.

- Take advantage of features such as multi-touch gestures, Apple Pencil support, and professional-grade editing tools to bring your ideas to life.

8. Virtual and Augmented Reality (AR):

- iOS 17 introduces innovative AR experiences that blur the line between the digital and physical worlds.

- Explore AR apps and games that transform your surroundings into immersive virtual environments, allowing you to interact with virtual objects and characters in real-time.

- Discover educational, entertainment, and productivity apps that leverage AR technology to enhance learning, storytelling, and visualization.

Chapter 8

Troubleshooting and Maintenance: Keeping Your iOS 17 Device Running Smoothly

Maintaining the optimal performance of your iOS 17 device is essential for a seamless and enjoyable user experience. From troubleshooting common issues to performing routine maintenance tasks, here's a detailed guide on how to keep your iPhone or iPad running smoothly:

1. Restarting Your Device:

- If you encounter issues such as freezing, crashing apps, or unresponsiveness, restarting your device can often resolve the problem.

- Press and hold the power button (or the power button and volume down button for iPhones without a physical home button) until the power-off slider appears.

- Slide the slider to power off your device, then press and hold the power button again to turn it back on.

2. Updating iOS:

- Keeping your device up to date with the latest iOS version is crucial for security patches, bug fixes, and performance improvements.

- Go to Settings > General > Software Update to check for and install any available updates.

- Ensure that your device is connected to Wi-Fi and has sufficient battery life before starting the update process.

3. Managing Storage:

- Running out of storage space can slow down your device and affect its performance. Regularly managing your storage can help optimize performance.

- Go to Settings > General > iPhone (or iPad) Storage to view a breakdown of your storage usage.

- Delete unnecessary apps, photos, videos, and files, and offload unused apps to reclaim storage space.

4. Clearing Cache and Data:

- Clearing cache and temporary data can free up storage space and improve performance, especially in apps that rely heavily on cached data.

- Go to Settings > Safari (or other apps) > Clear History and Website Data to clear browsing data in Safari.

- For other apps, check the app settings for options to clear cache or data.

5. Resetting Settings:

- Resetting settings to their default values can resolve issues related to misconfigurations or settings conflicts.

- Go to Settings > General > Reset and select "Reset All Settings" to reset all settings on your device.

- Note that this will not delete your data, but it will reset preferences such as Wi-Fi passwords, wallpaper, and accessibility settings.

6. Managing Background Apps:

- Background apps can consume system resources and drain battery life, impacting device performance.

- Double-click the Home button (or swipe up from the bottom of the screen on devices without a physical home button) to view recently used apps.

- Swipe up on an app's preview to close it and remove it from the background.

7. Monitoring Battery Health:

- Battery health degradation can impact device performance over time. Monitoring battery health can help you identify when it's time for a replacement.

- Go to Settings > Battery > Battery Health to view the maximum capacity and peak performance capability of your battery.

- If the maximum capacity is significantly degraded, consider replacing the battery through Apple's battery replacement program.

8. Seeking Professional Assistance:

- If you encounter persistent issues or hardware-related problems, it may be necessary to seek professional assistance.

- Contact Apple Support or visit an Apple Store or authorized service provider for diagnosis and repair services.

www.ingramcontent.com/pod-product-compliance
Lightning Source LLC
Chambersburg PA
CBHW050237230526
45470CB00005B/1988